The Blueing Hours

Albert DeGenova

VIRTUAL ARTISTS COLLECTIVE

http://vacpoetry.org

ISBN-13 978-0-9798825-3-1

ISBN-10 09798825-3-2

Special thanks to the following journals and anthologies for first publishing some of the poems in this collection: *After Hours*, "Skirts," "Dissonance," "Layers," "Long Lake," "Strong Legs," "The Cold Towing," "Orphaned," "What Dies With Me," "What if" and "Weathering"; *Blood Lotus.org* (Online literary journal), "Condemned"; *ChicagoPoetry.com* (Online anthology), "American Lost Soul"; *Clark Street Review*, "Nighthawks"; *E-poets.net* (audio readings), "Do You Know What It Means To Miss New Orleans," "On Coronado Beach" and "Feed Me"; *Free Lunch* (forthcoming), "They Danced"; *Paterson Literary Review*, "Chicken Shack Blues" and "Family Album"; *Lips* (forthcoming December 2008), "That Day a Man"; WBEZ (Chicago Public Radio) *"I want to be poet laureate" Contest*, Honorable Mention, "On Memorial Day."

The poems "American Lost Soul," "To Jimmy Santiago Baca," "Nighthawks," and "Living History" were included in the poet's book Back Beat (co-authored with Charles Rossiter) published by Fractal Edge Press. The poem "Angel" was included in the same collection as part of a longer poem titled "Angels Got The Blues."

For Cole and Max,
and to Eden who is my life

Table of Contents

The Blueing Hours

"Ah, it was a fine night, a warm night, a wine-drinking night, a moony night, and a night to hug your girl and talk and spit and be heavengoing. This we did."

Jack Kerouac, *On the Road*

The Red Hours

Do you know what it means
to miss New Orleans?

Downstairs my son plays boogie woogie
Professor Longhair Dr. John
New Orleans-style stride piano.
It is Mardi Gras week.
He's practicing for those
Fat Tuesday parties.
His foot stomps on the floor,
vibrates through the walls and up
to my desk. My head sways in time
to the rhythmic pulsing of his left hand
the dizzying parade of his right
sends serious thought into a funky pirouette
puts a smile on my face a reminder
of that old bouncing gait, of Bloody Marys
and Hurricanes mixed with rum and trumpets
and street dancers with bottle-cap taps on their shoes
a reminder of what this kind of blues can do
to a Dad who knows his son knows nothing
of Lenten sadness, only the joy of dancing,
a Dad who knows his own success
through the songs his son chooses to play –
Big Chief, Stagger Lee, Tippy Tina,
Laissez les bons temps rouler!

To-Do List

Because I question which white is true white
whether in ink or paint or fabric or paper
I still don't know the difference between
winter white and summer white,
eggshell, ivory, linen, and bone.

Because I question, the more
I question, the more
the definitions blur, the more
my young son's note to himself
sheds the clearest light of all…

Max's To-Do List
1. Call Grampa
2. Go to bed
3. Wake up

Strong Legs

On your seventieth birthday
face to face, standing firm
we shake hands, barely
warm as yesterday's toast.

•

I accepted your excuses then
you always absent from my sidelines –
you on your own cross-country run
somewhere, did you ever
look over your shoulder.

Though you bought me
orange bobbers and shiny lures
you never learned to tie a knot
or bait a hook
the nightcrawlers between us
stretch for miles.

•

I couldn't forgive
your car fire-bombed in front of our apartment building;
the incessant ringing of the black rotary phone
you directing me to answer, say
my Daddy isn't home;
after a night of scotch and water your almost bragging
about your new car with bullet holes in the fender;

———

the repo man in the alley hiding between garbage cans;
state troopers at the door with court summonses...
is your father home?
You never were.

Forgive?
outside the Inn Motion Ballroom where I was a bus boy
your friend signaling to shoot the driver of a car that
pulled up next to us, I remember *2:13 a.m.*
there was a bank clock across the street,
you stood firm,
you signaled *No* –
who were you protecting?

•

While your car burned, I
slept soundly in my warm bed.
Full belly.
You provided
in your way.

•

Today is so far from then
as I walk up a mountain trail
my son on my back when he,
short of breath, cannot go on;
as I hike down the Rio Grande gorge
never missing a step
like a pack mule

———

carrying my family's belongings –
I thank you
for these thick, short
Italian peasant legs.
Today at 44
I am somehow grateful
for you not teaching me about these legs
for hiding their strength.
Your absence was my teacher.
I look across this New Mexican mesa
across an ancient gorge, a horizon wider
than the scope of my eyes
a world out of man's scale
standing on your legs.

Angel

Max does a cartwheel dance
across the dewy grass
through a fog
that wraps us in springtime.
The clouds
Max says, *have come down to play*
to pinch our cheeks to tickle our ears
He is a four-year-old guardian angel
new at the job and always giggling.
Look, above the broccoli trees,
there's an accordion moon playing 'bye, bye, my baby
bye, bye' and I
am going to eat
colors
sunrise cereal
don't even try to stop me!
He pulls me through his playground
where jungle gyms are fantastic submarines
where red tulips stretch and scratch their bellies
and rocking horses play under umbrellas
where flying is as simple as letting go the swing.

Celebrating Solstice

Holding opposite ends
of a string of Christmas lights
we parade around the fir tree
transplanted into our living room
for this month of Santas
and snowmen and red ribbons.
Something deliciously pagan –
so primal – where are the bonfires,
the drums, women shimmying
in flickering shadows?
We toast and sing to birth
in the cold air of a dying season,
the dark solstice, so like
the hunter facing a wolf,
something deliciously alive
in the taste of death,
deliciously arousing
in our Christmas lights tug-of-war
across our selfish flames, the balancing
of air and earth, fire and ice,
our ritual dance of kiss and bite.

Skirts

You model your new gown
like a little girl playing dress-up
fancy high-heeled shoes but no hose
no party make-up, no contact lenses
you spin to see your black skirts whirl
swirling black satin, black
as moonless night, black
as sweat and sex and wisps
of musky hair
exposed as you raise your arms above your head
free, shameless
dancing your mambo to unheard rhythms
black as Puerto Rico's midnight beaches.

I close my eyes to your satin playfulness
and see a younger woman who danced
this same dance … eyes smiling
eyes staring into mine as red skirts swirled
and whirled around us, the same eyes.

I breathe in your musk your dance
your energy your black dress
remembering that first dance
that red dress, that fire dance in my heart
still.

Cézanne Jelly and Paper Kites

in our Cézanne season when reason was treason
blue was the color for days and nights
jelly on crackers the Tao of our Zen

the then of amen again and again
undulating shadows red lava light
that Cézanne season when reason was treason

sunshine like thunder begun and undone
purple and yellow crepe paper kites
jelly on crackers the Tao of our Zen

you were the one the one the one
to bless the black cat with child sight
a Cézanne season when reason was treason

I painted poems with naked pen
to remember black coffee mornings and nights
jelly on crackers the Tao of our Zen

and now our cold toes touch almost like then
when we danced in crackling firelight
that was our season when reason was treason
jelly on crackers the Tao of our Zen

American Lost Soul

1.

Mustang Sally drives a minivan now
her butterfly tattoo
is a blurred purple moth.

Miles can't swing the blues trapeze
Sonny's crippled saxophone hangs from the ceiling
my toe taps too late, and too often
not at all.

The remains of Jimi's guitars
cleansed of fire and outrage
decorate restaurants from coast to coast.

Louie Prima still sings, *A woman is a woman,*
and a man ain't nothin' but a man
but I just can't make sense of the lyric
anymore.

My old hangouts are pinned to a clothesline –
friends fade
haunted sheets in dying sunlight.

Canvas of test patterns
can't finish
the picture
anymore.

2.

Guards x-ray my shoes at the airport. My shoes!

I watch Oswald's murder.
I watch a plane fly into a building.
I watch wars like re-runs.
I watch my sister go blind.
I watch my son choke on a lollipop.
I watch a man play golf not 24 hours after burying his wife.
I eat hummus slowly searching for bones with my tongue.
I watch the fire go out, the kindling
is ash.

I stand bare-chested
the rain against my face
black iron fire escape under my shoeless feet
rancorous fists pulling at wet hair
taunting the lightning –

I dare you
nothing
touches me
anymore.

Chicken Shack Blues

We were to play together
a gig, father and son
sax and piano
like some modern-day notion
of vaudeville, or
talent night at the PTA.
I taught him a greasy
fried and dirty blues
like teaching him to tie a half-Windsor
or drink beer
or to live in the wilderness
with what we carried on our backs –
blues in G, that's what I said
anxious to relive some smoky jam session memory,
as if there were some
truth
in those 12 bars.
We'll learn Chicken Shack.
He said,
it's just a blues.
Just!
just
a blues
so nonchalant
as if there were nothing to it.
But at least
the first time he played
"Chicken Shack"
it was with

me –
my
tenor's voice
my
growling low G
a father playing the blues
for his son
opening the door
to free the red rooster
to feed the gray fox.

What Dies with Me

My G.I. Joe had no Barbie
no *hey Joe* Geisha beauty
no Ken to cook his dinner.
My Joe was a Marine
dressed in camouflaged fatigues
with a red raised scar on his hard
plastic cheek.

I picked a Marine
like my Dad, tougher
than the Army Joe in simple green.
My Joe was real man
a man's man
fingers molded in trigger position.
Alone in his pup tent
my Joe piled sandbags around
his machine gun, bandaged himself,
stuck his own I.V.
and bayoneted an enemy
who fit Joe's own brown boots.

I picked a Marine
like my Dad, who proved tougher
than me in my surplus field jacket
hair well over my collar
pockets filled with pipe and poems.

My G.I. Joe has served for forty years
in a footlocker in an attic

———

puffing Lucky Strike smoke rings into the dark.
I salute his broken rubber-band tendons
dry and brittle, unfixable amputee
arms and feet lost
to the corners of his collectible barracks
an inheritance my sons will never see.

On Memorial Day

I hear the radio reports,
nostalgia about Pearl Harbor
and imagine my son drowning in burning oil.
Dulce et decorum est
Pro patria mori
'Nam vets have told me of green and more green
they hated the smell of
green
and brown
brown ear necklaces
of running through trenches shooting at
darkness, of
a year of dysentery
dulce et decorum
I missed the draft by months
the fluke of a birthdate.

sweet and proper
so many Johnnies with their guns
faceless shadows
in napalmed jungles,
on street corners in green fatigues
fading frescoes on crumbling walls.
There is no
saving face.

dulce et decorum
I feel the choke of mustard gas
my lungs burning, the airways

swelling shut … turning blue, tears
turning red, turning red tears

a young woman touches
as if someone were touching back
traces a name, a sea of letters
engraved in cold black marble, touches
as if someone were touching back.
dulce et decorum
She leaves a pack of Lucky Strikes.
dulce et decorum
There was no luck.
dulce et decorum
I imagine my son drowning in burning oil.
dulce et decorum
Memorial Day
the requiem is all the same,
the pain goes
            marching on

Living History

Hemingway's breath still lingers
here on this street, my street,
his street.
Did he ever walk across
my lawn, sit on my porch
on his way to school, the same school
my sons sit in now?
I walk past his boyhood home,
look up to his third-floor bedroom.
The light is on tonight in that center window.
Whose 17-year-old shadow
contemplates the glory of war?
Do those old floorboards still hold
the crescent moons of his fingernails?
If matter and energy can never be destroyed,
then history is a fishbowl –
we share this same water for eternity.
The song Hemingway hears
as he runs to catch a football
is my voice, my son's piano from our open door –
then, if it's all true
I swim in the same salty Mediterranean
where my grandfathers wash their feet.
I touch the skin of the dead then,
when I write my name in the dust
on my brother's Manhattan bookshelves
and the dead know me, know I am
here – now – trying to taste
their history like a ripe plum

_____

like sour mash, like
all the lovers who've kissed my lover's lips.
We are the ancient dirt beneath our feet,
are the Nazis, the Popes, the Michigan militia
all the hot dog vendors of Bourbon Street,
we are the President, we are the bombs,
the dead babies, the homeless garbage eaters,
we are history –
the waiter delivers our fathers' tabs,
and we pay, we pay.

What if

Daddy Daddy, I
focus
focus on his eyes
his eyes already
six years old
old.

Daddy Daddy, I
try try
to stop this moment to
hold it know it squeeze it
in my fist but watch it ooze
ooze through my fingers and
drip
drip
onto the carpet.

Daddy Daddy I
am
my my Max my Max
I am not thinking not
thinking of what to do
do next, I
promise I am not going to
not going to consider
what if
I am going to cherish this
face this face his
sunflower face.

Daddy Daddy I
listen
listen to his words
one by one by one by
one word at a time and
hope hope
to stop
time
just
this
one
time
this
one

The Black Hours

Nighthawks

This is the kind of night
when you notice
that the green neon buzzes a minor 7th
to the hissing whisper of the orange *Diner*
letters cracked with black, the kind
of night
when your wet jacket won't hang
on its hook,
when the fly
that shares the sugar on the rim of your coffee cup
has more to say than the cracking of your knuckles
stretched back against the sticky edge of the table
or the scratch
scratch of your pencil as it moves
across the margins
of this morning's paper. This is

the kind of night that writes
jazz-blues graffiti in low clouds lit
by amber streetlights, the ones that have yet
to burn out –
this night is
an empty ketchup bottle,
a fallen salt-shaker,
a dollar-ninety-nine breakfast special

the kind of night
when heaven

is a stained waitress
who's worked the night shift for seventeen years
the angel that makes the toast,
the only angel
on a night like this

Dissonance

A small move
    white key to black
one half-step forward or back
    colors major with minor
the smallest distance
    between piano keys
transforms gospel to blues
    Mozart to Monk.

The twitch of a muscle
    sounds a missed note
pinches the corners of a frown
    winks an eye
pronounces a wrong word
    brushes a finger against a cheek.

To think the end
    of a concerto hangs
precariously on the touch
    of one little finger as
delicately as an explanation
    between wife and husband
of the phone call
    that rings dissonance
the caller outside the chord.

A Son's Secrets

Precious is
a son
walking away
the brass knocker clank
the door closing behind him
yellow paper covered with
black words clenched
in a fist that will not open
to me
anymore.
It is
his
poem.

Precious are
a son's secrets
that lead him away
to his own decisions
and reasons and
rides in backseats
the stereo pounding
young women drumming rhythms
on smooth brown thighs
singing and laughing
all the way to the beach.
He builds his own sand castle.

There is a quiet dying
in me

for what he chooses not
to say.
His secrets become the man.

Precious is
the farewell
without a kiss.

Precious are
my secrets
the him
no lover will know
the him he will never be again –
the smell of his head after
a little league game,
the sound of his breathing
in a sleeping bag
next to me
birds singing us awake
two of us in one small tent.

There is a quiet dying.

She Paints
for Gabriele Stich

"I heard an old maestro of the guitar say: 'The *duende* is not in the
throat: the *duende* surges up, inside, from the soles of the feet'."
– Federico Garcia Lorca

She faces the white
canvas, glacial before her
snow-blindness reaching across
the continents of this, her
studio, attic sanctuary
floor to ceiling windows
sun-filled skylights
she faces the white
raises a long wide brush
awkward fencer, closes
her eyes for the first thrust
of orange acrylic, moving
now agile, spritely she
feels the weight of wool
sweater and lace beneath
fall away
as orange flows into yellow into
green strokes of long passage
beyond the slow running
drips of black black
she grips the stiff frame
holding the wetness
of color against her
nakedness swirling greens

---

and burnt umber of pelvis
into the slow kiss
of nipples against blue
blue
cobalt blue
she
has yet to move

the white of line one
stares its condescending glare
blank unspoken metaphor
not unlike the black angel that
lives inside her pillow, the lingering dream
whispering mortality, *duende* and then –

the first breath, the slow stroke
deliberate, driven
by the tickle and burn
of a fearless raw sienna smudge
unwashed, under her left breast.

Family Album

These are pictures of my family –
smell the garlic sautéed in olive oil
and poured over blanched escarole greens,
the stale air of trans-Atlantic steerage
fused with the sweat and bad breath
the rotting teeth of *Napolitain* poverty,
the oily coal smoke that replaced
sea air, forever,
the long train ride New York to Chicago,
one way.

These are pictures of my family –
fading color slides in plastic sleeves
that account for a decade, the 1950s
the fulcrum years
when my family teetered between
the slum streets of Naples and
southside Chicago unpaved alleys and
suburban subdivisions.
My grandparents with enough English to
play with their grandchildren, my young American parents who
never spoke their parents' language to each other.
We are the babies.

These are pictures of my family –
eating and smiling, singing *happy birthday day*
preserved in plastic just like Grandma's sofa ...
the sofa that discolored anyway, the streets that were paved,
we grew up, those who remembered Ellis Island

have been buried.
We are no longer guinea dock rats, we are no longer
sweating dark-skinned immigrants, we no longer
dig the ditches for Chicago sewers, no longer
lay the bricks of the city's skyline.

These are pictures of
my family.
I breathe these pictures into my lungs
and smell my grandfather's cigar,
his wine press and the emptied oak barrels.

My sons read this family album like a textbook,
the dry branches of a family tree, the sterile history
of lineage.
My sons will never know what an Italian smells like.

We are become
Americans with Italian names
tossing old country phrases
bocci balls that
miss the mark.

Orphaned

There is a wickedness in this place
fetid hallways reek of fish and dirty pennies
scarred mirrors only cloud the face

of a rusted clock in unaccounted space
while wallpaper crumbles with a parched disease –
there is a wickedness to this place.

All silence now up the tired staircase
no wailing or complaining, no demands to be appeased
scarred mirrors tend to cloud the faces,

yellowed photos, Mother and babies without embraces.
Cracked windows and hardened words allow a chilling breeze
there is wickedness in this place.

Grown daughter advances with a broken pace
while death is announced in a lonely wheeze
scarred mirrors only cloud the face

of mother in her shroud of green lace
whose veiled reasons are lost with her keys –
there is a wickedness in this place
scarred mirrors always cloud the face.

They Danced

My parents danced
that's what they did
all they did
well
together.
Swingin' 'til the lights came on!
And when they remarried
neither
married a dancer.
Sometimes you get the best
the first time around –
even if it's only on the dance floor
with the saxes, the cymbals, the dance wax,
even if the song
is only five minutes long.

To Jimmy Santiago Baca,
in the House Tonight

The open-mic graffiti poets posture
for the Buddha, master in the audience.
He listens, applauds, drinks
bourbon.
But tonight
words swirl around the writer's head
like ice cubes in his glass, like
updrafts of circling snow outside.
He asks me to play,
play my saxophone
a song for his brother
the brother who died
just winter days ago.

Play a song for me, play
a song for my brother
who was murdered.
Play a song because
there are things in a life
that you can't get over.
My mother was murdered
my father was murdered
and now
my brother —
there are things in a life
that you cannot get over.

He closes his eyes to say this,
he kisses his hands held as in prayer.
Faith in the Virgin of Guadeloupe,
better than the trigger I pulled
the cold blood I shed
angry lives ago.

My fingers find the keys, stumble
into "Amazing Grace"
and spiral into a freefall of blue notes
that is a dead brother.
There are things in a life
you cannot get over,
things
that make
this poet's poems.
No burning need
for an open microphone
or polite applause
only the request
for a song
this January night –
there are things in a life
you cannot get over.

The Kraftbrau Poetry Slam

(June 24, 2003, Kalamazoo, Mich.)

A farmer's daughter works the door
collects the open mic cover charge
and sells organic produce
giving away samples of sweet peas
and deep red strawberries.
Affecting a Japanese hostess,
she wears a gold silk dress, tight,
with slits up both ripe thighs
with slits
that open wider to smooth white hips, wider
with every bend of her knee
with each step up to the stage
where she reads her poems of coming
of age, of the poet who was her deepest lover.

Later, after the slammers empty their rage
into pints of beer and buckets of longing,
I ask the smiling farmer's daughter
what one would find under her soft silks,
she answers
metaphors
and I buy a two-dollar bag of strawberries
because this poem is not about sex, this poem is
about the freight train that passes outside the open window
that steals the words from our mouths,
that rumbles darkly into this long thick summer night.

Signed, Lonely in Dortmund

An archetype of smoke and beer
and moth-eaten sound systems,
the *Superfly* bar in Dortmund, Germany –

I am a cracked chromium nightmare
in the broken men's room mirror
the misplaced English graffiti

misspells global metaphor
"*I'll schött mein bitch*"
"*Dizsco Funk!*"

The live music is "trip-pop"
Euro mis-translation
of Miles Davis' fusion –

the 1970s bass funk groove
tight as yer ass pocket
don't mean anything in 2002.

I'm here with a
kissy-face B-movie couple
pregnant with their first

a girl, to be "Greta" like Garbo and maybe
she'll be an actress on some future
nightclub video screen or maybe not.

I sit on the last stool. The old cynic,
you see me in every corner tavern
in any wood-paneled pub

swilling beer
remembering when ...
tough to be lonely

if only
the barmaid made eyes
at me,

if only
the Creole singer *dame* crooned melancholy
sweet nothings to me, can't you see

if only someone cared to share
the scrapbook of empty matchbook covers
that fills my pockets

penciled scribblings of misty trysts
smudged with folding
and enfolding

Condemned

At a ranch in the dark hills outside of Las Vegas
girls lined-up in their tattoos and laces –
one whispered between giggles, *I always get the short ones.*
Later at the $4.99 buffet of the Seven Deadlies
we drank gasoline and smoked fat cigars
all for one and one for all musketeers
we called that years-ago night our *Original.*

Tonight Kentucky wives kick off their shoes
and wiggle their painted toes.
I sing Dr. John's prescription
for love and happiness
and me tokin' from a glass pipe
drinkin' warm bourbon –
It's a good thing we didn't have one more
she says, *leave the lights on*
I've never seen you before.

Enjoy my magic carpet ride little one, you
with your thumb up.

Sonnet Beyond Obsession

So where does this long pier
of night and endless dreams
lead us? Out, past the breakers,
past the harbor point, well past
the life guards and safety
of the marked swim area?
We walk bravely hand in hand
beyond obsession.
I see your face in my dinner espresso.
I see you naked tied to my headboard.
I see you topless bent over the bathroom sink.
I see you sunrise at my bedroom window.

We measure how far we've ventured
with syllables long and short.

That Day a Man

I walked with her
across the parking lot
up interminable stairs, into an elevator
whose doors slammed like God's gavel,
then a long green-white hall into room 301
where we waited. I held
her hand and held her
hand. She was my wife
then. I was a man
that day. And sad
then, our baby
then, she couldn't
handle this
not now she said, I didn't
know then
that clump
of cells was
probably
not mine.
Twenty-four years later I do
not judge that choice
of hers. But can't help considering
potential. What would
the missing one
have become. The two
sons I shake hands with
almost
men now, both
with eyes like mine.

Fulcrum

The clock above the kitchen sink
ticks the distance between us –
motionless black coffee
reflects nothing
the table is too wide
to reach the sugar
myself, it is
disappointment
the black hour, the negative
end of
balanced, this dark weight
is too heavy, pass
the sugar over the fulcrum
of this moment, a hand
on a knee, lean in
and out, we are
the up and down
the tick the tock
and all the hours in between.

The Blueing Hours

The Cold Towing

Frozen blue-white bean fields
no crows, no deer
no shadows
yet all is in shadow
this dawn in Indiana
bare trees with stiff
fingers caught in misty hair nets
the thermometer reads minus 8,
hint of sunlight orange-tinged
white jet tails like wisps
of breath hung high in the air
where something was –

nothing moves
save me
at 80 mph
alone on I-90 de-iced asphalt
driving into sunrise
with ten-thousand days in tow.

After Reading Neruda's *Twenty Love Songs* That Are Fewer Than Our Years Together

Tonight I write the saddest lines
in the small of your back where
it is wet from my tongue
my finger shaping letters
against the nap of your
soft down that resists the words
we have loved and not loved
we have joined and released
fire feeding earth, air
breathing water, we
are a thunderstorm of
flesh against flesh, tongue
to tongue to rain to
ice to lightning ignited
and smiles exploded
teeth heavy as sleet
shaping words that are not
love not love are love

tonight I write the saddest lines
that mark the hours
of sleepless darkness staring
you cannot read the silly
silhouettes of vowels traced along your spine
the long weary line of
sometimes you love me
with venom, sometimes
laughing, sometimes dancing

over broken stones, some-
times begging for the light
to be shut off, some-
times you love me with sleep

tonight I write in the small
of your back, tracing your hip
with exclamations and questions
and sad ellipses and lonely
empty spaces between
I and love and you
so many words
when all you ask is quiet

Layers

We shed
our layers of nakedness
over miles of years
and sheets lit by
nightlights in
corner sockets
and lava lamps that
move like you
to silent mambo rhythms
with enough light to almost
see
the outline of another
stripped skin left behind
until the last silks of histories slip
through the open window and
disappear
in undisguised sunlight.

Long Lake

(Phelps, Wisc., July 17, 2002)

wooden pier
creaks
under wet feet
footprints follow and
fade in sunlight
air buzzes with blue dragonflies
children chasing calling
from across the lake
a short blast of chainsaw
an empty rowboat bumping a
black tire nailed to the pier
man in a green motorboat
casts
reel whines
yellow lure plops
he focuses on the click of his line
silver chain stringer slaps
the aluminum hull
sad splashing of dying catch
a baby cries
a father scolds *put that down Alex*
from inside a white cottage, a vacuum cleaner
drags itself to work
moaning and puffing its bag of dust
cigar ash hits the water
hiss …
I relish the quiet that is not

silence,
scribble this,
note my path of
dry footprints
write ... there is no past
to this
present tense.

Feed Me

Feed me
your blackberries
soaked in rain or sweet white cream
in a flaming brandy sauce
in your belly button
down the zipper of your jeans
balanced on the pucker of your lips
in between your toes
spread like jam over your breasts –
I eat you blackberry
bitter or sweet.

After Dinner

And this is what I am
all the things of my pockets
held in cupped hands
as if to splash my face
with pictures of my sons,
a cell phone, a pipe and
poems, car keys, a bit of lint, a
twenty-dollar bill

as if these things
could clear my head, this dream
palms cradling a draft of silken honey – I dive
into the craggy shallows
of pockets, bruise my brow
on what was left there
a rubber band stretched thin
once loose around my wrist –
your restrained reminder.

Souring Metaphors

Crows line the horizon.
The milk in your breasts sours.
The piano is out of tune.
Your cheeks smell like mascara.
You walk through the valley of fear.
I fix the plumbing.
I carry the groceries.
You are the wind at the curtains.
I read suicide poems.
Your voice calls from a locked steel box.
I read without light.
You eat the leftovers.
You pull the weeds.
I smear gray ink.
You scream at the laundry.
You scream
at the laundry.

On Coronado Beach

(San Diego, California, September 8, 2003)

I imagine myself Picasso carrying a parasol
protecting his dark-haired beauty,
old man both master and servant
but there is no one under my umbrella, today.
I don't even have an umbrella.
I sit in the sand watching pelicans dive
beak first full speed into the Pacific.
I watch sailors run along the beach
up and back an endless circling parade.
I think I will never stand at the helm
of the sailboat that crosses this horizon.

At this moment I want more than anything
to tear off my trunks and dive into the waves
to wrap my nakedness in this womb of salt water
but I know I won't. I never have.

The woman who walks alone
ankle-deep splashing waves
will not talk to me.
I don't even say hello.
No Marilyn Monroe,
no passionate poetess,
no wife will appear from within the hotel bar behind me.
The back of her head had nothing to say.

I accept my place on this beach –
sand castle builder of dreams and fantasies.

I accept that wishing
like praying
never makes it so,
that the empty cup
forgotten in the sand will stay there
unless I move to pick it up
and whether I choose to fill it with sand or water
is what really makes all the difference.

Weathering
after Tom Waits

The day after tomorrow
I will die
the weather promises to be
clear, the day after tomorrow
our sons will read my few poems
and search for answers
as they pepper the wind with me
the day after tomorrow
they will be two days older
and I will not be buying lunch
proud Papa at LaPlayita Taqueria
but the sun may shine
as it did, the day before yesterday
when I cried my first morning cry,
that afternoon my mother made cookies
and yesterday, I remember now,
I laughed at the rain
that could not douse the campfire
under our pots – though it thundered.
But the day after tomorrow
I will be dead
and today I work
I measure time by the clouds
that pass in stocking feet
until tomorrow
when I will ride my bicycle
on the smooth path along Lake Michigan
yes, tomorrow will be a good day

———

I will drink a glass of red wine with you
tomorrow, but the day after –
I will be dead, certainly
no angel to roll back any stone
my last exhale will hang
like stale cigar smoke –
the weather may be clear
or not, no question.

Albert DeGenova grew up in Chicago and now lives with his family in Oak Park, Illinois. From 1978-1980 he was an editor of the *Oyez Review* (published by Roosevelt University); in June of 2000 he launched the literary/arts journal *After Hours,* for which he continues as publisher and editor. DeGenova is half of the performance poetry duo *AvantRetro* which appears throughout the greater Chicago/Midwest area. His book, *Back Beat* (a collection of poetry combined with memoir tracing the influences of the Beat movement on two contemporary poets), was co-authored with poet Charles Rossiter and published by Cross+Roads Press in 2001 (a second edition was released in June 2006 by Fractal Edge Press). Of *Back Beat,* Lawrence Ferlinghetti wrote, "*Back Beat* beats everything for being beater than the Beats." DeGenova received his MFA in Writing from Spalding University, Louisville. He is a blues saxophonist and one-time contributing editor to *Down Beat* magazine.

" i can see that"

Acknowledgments

I'd like to express my deep gratitude to all those who have encouraged, critiqued, and supported the work in this book. But I'd like to especially thank Rane Arroyo, teacher and friend, who was instrumental in the shaping, editing, and organizing of the original manuscript that has evolved into this book. Rane's encouragement and belief in my poetry has made the difference that only a few can know. Who would have known in 2005 that his suggestion for a chapter name would become the title of this collection.

Creating the perfect atmosphere for this book are the photographs of Herb Nolan. Thank you Herb, your pictures give my words air to breathe.

Also, a huge thank you to my Chicago "workshop" partners and friends whose insights helped finish many of the poems in this book: Larry Janowski, Patricia McMillen, Nina Corwin, and Charlie Rossiter.

To my best, longest and closest personal editor Pat Hertel, thank you for everything you do.

And to Steven Schroeder and the Virtual Artists Collective, this book would not be possible without your belief in my poetry. Thank you.

Printed in the United States
218909BV00001B/6/P